The Futurist's Mistress

To Harriet —
with love!
Love, Larry

The Futurist's Mistress

by Lorraine Schein

Mayapple Press 2006

Published by MAYAPPLE PRESS
408 N. Lincoln St.
Bay City, MI 48708
www.mayapplepress.com

ISBN 0-932412-39-4

ACKNOWLEDGMENTS

Grateful acknowledgment is made to the editors of the following magazines and anthologies in which some of these poems first appeared: *Astropoetica, Asylum, Bay Windows, The Beltane Papers, Blueline, Broken Mirrors, Brooklyn Review, Dreams and Nightmares, Exquisite Corpse, Full Unit Hookup, Furious Fictions, Gargoyle, Heresies, Home Planet News, IKON, Poetry New York, Rattapallax, Red Tape, Semiotext(e) SF, Space and Time, Starline, Terminal Velocities, Unbearables, We'Moon 2004* (Mother Tongue Ink), *Women Artists Datebook 2005* (Syracuse Cultural Workers), *Xenophilia* and elsewhere.

Cover design by Judith Kerman based on a rubber-stamp collage by Lorraine Schein

Book designed and typeset by Judith Kerman in Calisto MT text; all titles in Lucida Sans Demibold Italic.

Contents

"In her dreams palpable and other coordinates exist, not always interfering with each other..."

—*Luisa Valenzuela*

Map of Tuesday

Sleeping westward,
we fall through the doors of the sky
a hand comes out from a cloud
and folds the air
into small winds
that pass like memories.
Somewhere in the distance
night's black telephones are calling—
pick up the phone pick up the phone
at the other end, I hear my own voice speak:
a silence waiting for a silence.

The Crystal World

after J.G. Ballard

And then
We saw
How we
Had been transformed:
The sky was striped chalcedony,
Our eyes, dark periwinkling chatoyancies,
Irised amethysts, creviced amethysts.
The trees had branches
Of malachite and obsidian,
Leaves heavy with humming green tourmaline
That processed the light.
Your hair was smoky quartz and amber
Veined with carnelian and capillaries of garnet.
The crescent moon was a dark tiger's-eye—
The sun, reverted to moonstone
Set in peridot.
The sea, a slow-seething lava mass
With blue cliff breakers
Of lapis lazuli, drusy chrysacolla,
Ultra-sound turquoise and gold-streaked azurine.
The air was clear quartz—
White coral was the intricate wind
And coldly carving.
Your kunzite hand on my amazonite breast
Of beryl-tipped opal...
Your kiss held a topaz desire, was
Jasper with passion.
Your profile, an astral cameo.
Your voice, clairaudient.

Divulgences

Matter is actually composed of infinitely
Teeny whirring helicopters.
Don't tell the physicists—what do they know?
Not much.
Thought-forms are a sort of fairy.
Also, elementals and pookas.
Silkies are sea creatures by day
And turn into men and women at night.
And all fairies live in caves.
Millions of dreams clipped daily;
Millions of dreams clipped daily.
We are pushing the water—
Push the water, push it
Till it breaks open and lets you in and through
Its liquid revolving door
Into the shattering at the heart of
Its most hidden wave.

The Garden of Time

After a painting by the Surrealist artist Eileen Agar

Here, an atomic clock blooms chronons.
Nuclear pistils strike and quiver at the hour.
The bright petals of minutes enfold me.

A Cesium fountain spouts an arc of atoms
resonating with distant stars
that spread like weeds.

A sundial, growing profusely in the shade,
cross-pollinates a digital clock's electric blue numbers.
A nanosecond flowers into eternity.

Green horological splicings
oscillate hybrid pendulums.
Greenwich Mean Time droops on the vine.

Dinosaur seedlings sprout into
paleontologic remnants of the future.
A fossil plant turns its bony head from the moon
to watch us extinct.

Delphic (Projection #3)

The futurist's mistress
(In this alternate scenario)
Sleeps in his bed,
Beside his other curved concubines,
Space and Time.

She projects herself, once more,
Endlessly into his future.

The dreams crash and glisten;
Presaging a love
More fantastic than science—

The futures tighten around her
like his arms in the night.

Alien Cities

The city inside a star,
The city inhabited by black machines—

The city of dreaming robots,
The city of women astronauts—

The futurists' city,
The city built of rain—

The city whose sky is filled with artificial moons,
The city that appears each midnight and disappears each noon—

The flying city, built on a comet,
The city run by psychic children—

The city of the exploding sun,
The city of architectural perfection—

And the city that we stand in now,
Strange as all the rest—

If we could but see it
With alien eyes.

Dream Pillow 1

Her dream pillow was inducing too many dreams. Some of them were lucid enough to escape and got caught by the dream catcher over her bed, which scooped them up and netted them back into the pillow like basketballs through a hoop, where their scents mingled with its lavender, mugwort and hops.

Several of them gave off the powerful stench of nightmares, burning flesh and sulphur—others had the mild, pleasant lemony laundry-like odor of everyday dreams. The lucid ones smelled like the smoke of lit molten glass; the sexual ones of musk, sweat and smegma. But the precognitive dreams were the worst. They smelled of decayed, screaming black hole roses.

She ripped her pillow open and all her trapped dreams spilled out in a profusion of smell, image, and noise. She opened the window wider to set them free and air the room.

One of them got caught in her hair, though, and became reality.

Dream Pillow 2

If I put this tiny pillow
Under my large one
Will I dream of smelly, flattened small pillows?

Dream Pillow 3

Shards of glass, barbed wire, three golden nose rings, a lock of platinum hair for a punk pillow;

A policeman's finger, a priest's erection, a prison key for an anarchist pillow;

A caught swirl of water, a butterfly in a storm, a poet's random midnight jottings for a chaos pillow.

Heracleitus Warp Variants

Time sings to itself and smells of space.

It is a blind child, playing in the dark,
A little girl, shy but swift
Racing past worlds unseen.

Her sister is Fate, her mother Silence.
When she walks, she grasps the hand of Eternity.

She plays tag with photons
And jacks with the planets,
Gathering them up in one hand. Time is Queen
Of all games.

Time is a child lost in her own thoughts.
Her favorite color is music.
We are her dolls; she touches our faces and leaves her marks

And then she puts us to bed.

Alpha Ralpha Boulevard

In memory: Cordwainer Smith

Half-cat, she
Walks with me
Up onto that heartbreaking arc, that road that
Curves into the sky.
Its arch disappears into white cloud, high.

Below us, the city
soon becomes tiny.
It glitters in the sun
like golden microcircuitry.

When finally we come down
Onto the other side,
I, too, will be half-animal—

Lost, this path's roused memories
Of the lucid dreams of science,
The sleepwalked road of human history.

Concocted Prophecy

Foreplay with the ephemeris
Produces precognitive moments.
A sustained level of digital stimulation
Is necessary for destiny's arousal.
Lubrication of astrolabes
Does not necessarily indicate readiness for intercourse.
An asteroid plugging up vagina and anus
Is sometimes necessary to reach orgasm.
The G-spot is an area
Corresponding to the constellation Cygnus.
It may take the horoscope some time
To learn how to stimulate itself manually.
Masturbation is more satisfying, exalted in the eighth house
When done by horary astrology.
All bodily functions speed up
As the star systems become pre-orgasmically flushed,
Reddening with fire as vasocongestion begins.
The future will be an orgasmic contraction of your natal chart
That climaxes every 0.8 seconds.

Dorothy's Poem

The long, gray hair of the rain had fallen.
She slept on the old down comforter of the sky.
When she woke up,
she dreamt that her house was flying,
that a witch rode by—
past the clouds, on a bicycle.
Where was the air going?
The wind poured out from her eyes.

Auto-Cento of Looking Glass Shards

Shatterings of a poem by Lewis Carroll from Through the Looking Glass

Echoes fade and memories die;
Summer was a fad, but so am I.

Autumn frosts have slain July—
Now winter scrapes against the sky.

Still she haunts me, phantomwise,
Especially the memory of her fey thighs, oh

Alice, moving under skies
Hair suffused with clouds and sighs,

The toys of time, its snuffling cries, child
Never seen by waking eyes—

My dream's pupil darkens;
The rest is a lie:

And wonder: why, and why and why...

Lady Twilight

Some fairy women can never be seen—no mortal's heart is that pure.
The fairies choose who will see them: in this green dusk I see a door

between the worlds, where Lady Twilight wraps the West
in her gray mantle of fine mist.

She holds a goblet of lake water that darkens,
reflecting the May Eve moon.

Voices behind her call my name, and hands reach out for me
from a world made of yearning, a world now possible to see.

This is the dangerous time: when the *sidhe*
can trespass into our reality.

Most women die when seized with longing for fairy things—
but a few are taken to Tír-na-n-Óg to dance with fairy kings.

[Note: *Sidhe* is the Gaelic word for fairies, and is pronounced "shee"]

The Dark of the Matter

Tara, the astrophysicist at the Institute for the Unknown, had finally isolated the universe's dark matter and put it in a bottle to see what it was made of. She poured it out into a beaker and subjected it to a battery of tests.

First she tested it for hidden spirals, then for magic rituals to see if it was made out of the new moon. Indefinite findings. She probed it with thin silver instruments for poetry, with some success, for it started to mumble short, enigmatic verses that she recognized as Japanese death haiku, those haiku composed by Zen masters on their deathbeds. She passed colored beams of light through it, but this only intensified its darkness.

Finally, as she was about to leave the lab for the day, she heard it sigh contentedly, like a child folded in the womb, and go to sleep.

And this gave her the first clue that led to her theory and subsequent published paper on its composition.

6.3 Synchrons

"When two or more events take place at a given moment of time without either one having caused the other but with a distinctly meaningful relationship existing between them beyond the possibilities of coincidence, that situation has the basic elements of synchronicity. . . . The essence of Synchronicity is to be found in the fact that Synchronicity carries a principle of orderedness that occurs in the universe regardless of causal connections and beyond space and time."

—*Jung,* Synchronicity and Human Destiny

This is a synchronicity chart, assembled using data from our tracking devices, detailing the synchrons that co-manifested at precisely 22:52 Western Galactic Time, at Spacelab 423, Multi-Dimensional Scanner Project of the Synchronics Lab, Special Monitoring Division:

1. The White City of Aeoll, which had reduced itself to a size capable of being balanced on a human fingernail, shatters as its micro-moon reaches syzygy.

2. The clear green moonlight of New Manhattan shines seriously and coldly down through a curved glass wall, casting dappled jade shadows onto the bare body of the woman sleeping within. She hears the noise of something breaking in her dream, and awakes, startled. But everything is silent around her. Poised in stillness. She gets up, and presses the auditory activating button for the sound of an autumn wind during a rainstorm on Earth. Soon she is asleep again, and the shadows are back in place.

3. A ray of light, emitting from 23° 4' of the right side of the Zetrian crystal, lights up the southwest corner of Dr. P.'s desk.

4. The EEG pattern on the chart of Moira Robinson, a woman whose dreams are being monitored, shows an irregular and inexplicable REM pattern, unprecedented in the knowledge of the Sleep Lab researchers.

5. A sub-telepathic thought about how rain is always lucky for her, barely perceptible by her conscious mind, causes the woman walking past the Sleep Lab to continue on her way instead of

taking shelter from the impending thunderstorm. This leads to her unplanned meeting with the transcriber of this chart.

6. Thrown impatiently by a young poet who lives on the outskirts of the space colony, the I Ching forms Hexagram 22 (Beauty).

6.3 *Co-manifestation/Transcausal Element:* Plink. The noise of the Ninth Dimension revealing itself, the sound of the pebble of Space thrown into the water of Time picked up by our sensitized devices, unfurling, a rift permanently opened in space-time by it, a kite of ineffable dimensions soaring through itself, tugging at its own string.

The Queen of Velcro

The Queen of Velcro is fuzzy and black on one side, and has sharp plastic teeth on the other. Her lovers are kept in a state of suspense, never knowing which side of her to please. But the truth is, she can only achieve satisfaction by pressing each opposing side of herself against the other till they adhere, then attaining release as she pulls herself apart in a long, ripping sigh.

Nikola Tesla

Nikola Tesla,
inventor of radio,
fluorescent lighting,
the alternate current generator
(and secret futuristic machines
we can only guess at now),

liked to watch lightning storms
as he lay on his black mohair couch
muttering to himself all the while
of *what* and *how*.

He could test machines by visually
running them in his mind
and then looking to see
if there were any flaws he could find.

He had a mind like a bolt from the blue—
indeed, some said
he was really a Venusian who
had fallen to Earth.

And Tesla was cracked as lightning, too:

He liked: pigeons and poetry
and numbers divisible by three,
counting his steps as he walked,
and estimating the amount of food
in each dish of his meals, cubically.

He disliked, violently:
earrings on women
(especially pearl),
camphor's odor,
and of touching human hair
he had a great terror.

The mind is a strange machine
running on an alternate current—
rationally/irrationally,

the electricity of eccentricity,
the eccentricity of electricity—
who could have invented Nikola Tesla?

Mad as a scientist,
madder than poets—
mad; as we all are—

he saw the future by lightning,
while most of us don't even bother
to look up at it in the sky
and wonder what it really is,
and how, and why?

Bed

Dais of morning.
Relentless destination.
Ascension platform for astral travel.

Consciousness-sleeve.
Wrapped sculpture.
Cheapest living space.

Mammal's cave-floor digging.
Lightless trench in
the deep-sea floor.

Sleep raft for navigating
black-water eye movement rapids.
Private laboratory for self-experimenters.

Display box nesting
inside one larger,
boxed in night.

Lidless jewel case
previewing another cheap bauble
for Death's long fingers.

Sibylline Byte

Pythoness on time's tripod, three-eyed psychic camera, convulsing factoids, in her infotrance on snake hard drive. Random Access Memory. The fumes of the past-future were intoxicating. She sees Y2K, Y10K, Y100K, past all computers and information, Y1000K, where computers are made of light and synthetic neuron-skeins. The vapors envelop her, till she's a fragrance that shimmers, a fragrance from eons beyond unseen, and eons before. Her fangs sink deep, her venom cures . . . time's one-directionality.

Hissing sibylline cog. Concocted prophetess. Female vaginal orifice-oracle. Vagina whentata. How things fit together. Voids discovered. Chewing the laurel leaves of prophecy. Processing information at FTL-speed from other worlds. Directly accessing the motherboard. Words slithering from her mouth, ready to strike at sense. Routed from the technotemple by Apollo. But to return, avenge.

A labyrinth-circuit hangs by fiber optics over the entrance to her cavern, near twisting cables of water. Its code must be read correctly for entry.

"What do you want, sibyl?" asked the beings who succeeded, kept her alive and tortured her with their questions.

"I want to disconnect," she had told them many times, but they had just laughed and asked another question to contort her.

The Mask of Night

A sleep mask masks sleep so that it does not recognize and awaken her. But she can see it still, swirling under her eyelids, satin under the satin mask.

When she wakes up, a blind man is lying between her legs. His eyelids are sewn shut with her eyelashes. He says nothing, but reaches for her.

The Origami Universe

Fold the universe on unseen lines
Along a glistening crease of stars:
The cosmos, crimped along its three dimensions,
Its galaxies and spirals,
By skillful hands
Into a 4-D paper form,
The shape of space-time.
Pull out the hidden moons
Tucked in its corners
To rise, paper-white, over some new planet.

The Laser Light Girl

Light: The wands she sold were brighter than the snow, a colder light.

Amplification: She flipped one on—it flared open, a humming white door.

Stimulated by: Oscillation between energy levels and the subtle realms of matter.

Emission of: Coherent light waves, so she could see the dead and the not-quite existing.

Radiation: Electromagnetic—she saw her grandmother pulsing in the now-visible ultraviolet/infrared regions of the spectrum as she froze.

The First Three Minutes/Kabbala 3

I said, "All you have is this moment.
The twenty-first century's yesterday."
You said, "Let's swim to the moon, baby."

Time waves thunder over us
As we undress in our parallel universes.
I'm drowning in yours
I'm going down on yours
And you on mine
With the long fierce tongue of exploding suns
Licking at the swelling clitoris
At the center of my universe.

I'm aroused by the black lengths of Space, they make me super-
saturated—
The décolletage of those depths,
That endlessness clasped tightly around me,
Wearing black spandex and nothing else.
The farthest reaches embrace me.

Space plays with itself and swings all ways at once.
Space spreads her legs open to the approaching rocket.
But what she really wants is my hand up her black hole
And my tongue licking hard at the blue clitoris of flame
At the center of the universe
Bright tongue of fire
Tonguing the galactic clitoris, arousing its folds of void and
matter,
Licking itself into creation, as I lick it.

Oh faster faster
Past the speed of light—
Lick at the center of my universe
Till I catch, catch fire and burn
Throwing off arms of new matter around you.
Creation is conflagration and now I am, too.

And then the vision comes...
Above the vault of the heavens,
Are 955 domes
And, above them, the high and exulted throne
And above the throne,
A consuming fire
And His precious throne.
Oh, all His servants are fire!
And now I am fire on fire, flowered into fire,
And your servant, as you are mine,
Head still between my legs,
My throne, yours.

Fractal Fairytale

Once upon a time in the Land of Fractals there lived a family called the Sets. The father's name was Mandelbrot, the mother's name was Julia, and their baby's name was Chaos. One morning while they were eating breakfast, they noticed a scientist watching them. Baby Chaos was afraid, but his mother told him to just go on eating his cereal and being random.

Level Five

Slashing
still upward
gaping
lurches of distance
gasping magnitudes
beyond
the six directions of space,
we carved onto and
grappled
a new level
made of the root of all velocity
an empty whiteness, filled
with no planet, and
with no name—
only the shock of pure realm
and the sound of
angels screaming.

Alien Girl: From the 11th

You can tell she's one. She comes from another planet. Where eyes are clairvoyances, mouths are vortexes of voices. Where it is always night. Where one whirls, not walks; implodes, not talks.

She got here by illegally crossing the borders between hypnogogic sleep and subliminal waking REM. She sews tiny mirrors in the hems of her skirts that she peers at, to make sure her face and legs are still there. What are breasts for? What is the cavity between her legs for? Her hair is an uncontrolled substance.

Your thoughts are a contaminant to her. Stop thinking! Earth is decade-infested. All Earthens must be onzydecimated!

Thunder is the voice of the Eleventh Planet. She hears messages from home in lightning storms. She sees by remote-viewing. She is a spiritual emergency. The kundalini energies run through her brain and neurological system and sometimes burst out, catching onto Earthlings' spinal columns, an orgone-flame licking their third eyes ablaze.

She's told them about the discovery of her planet, in the ninth dimension, somewhere between sleep and autism. She tells them that reality is not only the exact opposite of what they say is true, it is what they have omitted. Like the Occult Masturbation of Comic Strips. Comic Strips being the medium for the secret revelatory parables of the Eleventh Planet, "The only way you Earthens will ever learn!" she yells as they put the jacket on, too tight. The Deeper Reality, occurring in the spaces between the panels, and the panels left out, the colors the papers don't even print in. The third-dimensional instead of the two. But at night, black holes open up in the word balloons, blooming in their empty spaces, uttering symbols in an inverted black language. Then you'll all get closer, closer to the Eleventh. You're just comics within comics, until you see the light, like Little Nemo and Dale Arden, peering around the edges of the frames that have always been their lives, seeing that there's more, there's other, that they've been lied to. Then the real story spills out, the real universe, from under the colored ink dots. But no one wants to believe; they climb back into their panels, ignore the sound and smell of the Eleventh—jasmine thrown into the heart of the sun, acrid jasmine-plasma.

She spends a lot of time in the white wards, the padded rooms. They take away all metallic objects from her: her pocket saucer, ion transporter in the shape of a silver lipstick and interstellar dream communicator. They can't take away her subliminal objects, because they can't see them. She tries to communicate to the base by autogenic sleep jerks. She tries to pick up messages by remote viewing of precognitions.

As a child, she always felt so different from everyone, she thought that would change when she got older. But she still feels that way. She's trying to escape, to create an alternate-reality tunnel through pinhole universes with bits of skin. An electric bulb filament, a match and her dermal surfaces, burrowing a hole into the web of extra ninth-dimensionality that's visible when the screaming starts.

The suicidal are really attempting to go home, to adjust to a foreign environment. Depressed females are just remembering where they've come from. The schizophrenically lonely are really stranded aliens.

But there is no way to contact the Mother ship. The Mother ship can't save her: it's left through a time-warp too subtle to follow, towards a new universe unimaginably far away.

Wings of Augury

My wings are driftwood,
For I have been a tree—
Wood that has dreamt in water
And emerges remembering, on the shore
As we dream, afloat in sleep's waters
Future drifting into past.

And I have been a hand
Holding high a sword,
Cutting hypnotic circles in a trance-smooth lake.

And I have been a black stone in the moonlight
And a dancer among black stones,
Dancing to black starlight.

A golden torque and vervain crown I wore then,
On the Druidess Isle of the White Maidens.

These things sacred to all priestesses:
Water, stone and tree.
The sea is an omen of the shell.
The shell augurs the sea.

Fortunes can be read in fallen leaves
And in the white foam runes of the tide, where
Between their oracular duties and sweeping the sea floor
Begging for apples, the mermaids have often come ashore.

Sibyl of the Inner City

She is her own inner circle, circling. She lives alone in a fifth-floor, walk-up cave. The other side of her door is inscribed with a pentacle, scratched into the metal with a knife.

She tells the future from dirty city leaves, the veined rust on tin cans, the discarded clothes and sofas on the street.

Like all psychics, she predicts the present best—a shadow cast on moving water. Her clients believe her.

She wants to die to *their* world.

Outside, the city is a forest of lights, a sea of sound. And within her. "The great recluse lives in the city," she reads in her book on Chinese poetry.

She buys colored candles from the magic shop and powdered herbs for spells—mugwort, valerian, flying powder. Sometimes she makes her own scented oil, blending fixative, neroli, white jasmine, hyacinth and wild rose with a perfumer's funnel.

She wears only silver jewelry, a silver crescent pendant, snake spiral ring, silver hoop earrings.

Her lover is the moonlight cast onto her bed, rays mingling with the violet neon light from the sign across the way.

Her pelvis is an altar. Her altar today holds Tarot cards, white flowers, a small saint card from the botanica showing a smiling woman immersed in flames, a blue-veined marble found in the street.

She is a dormant riot of magical possibilities, the street's intersecting numinosities. She is a wiser, older density—an occult slum, the intensity of squalor and cunning, potentially eruptive with the tenacious secrets of the dark, ancient ones.

What she tells you is a burned page saved from an incinerator. She is a fragment you will try to reconstruct one day above the subway's roar.

Three Rains

It's raining here on New Earthport. I watch it fall past the circular windows that look onto the rocket bases; it looks just like the rain on Old Earth, even if it is artificially made. In my travels between the galaxies, I have seen rain on many different planets.

On Amphora 2, the capital city, Llelalia, is built of rain. It falls like liquid stalactites from the red-streaked sky, a clear tiara of sound, planned to the last droplet by the famous rain architects to form the shimmering tetrahelixial water pavilions. I remember hovering above those tall streaming domes in my ship, seeing the spaceflowers emerge. They unfolded like enormous intricate paper blossoms, only to immerse themselves slowly back into the flow of hyperspace.

The city smelled of the wild scent of the rain.

* * *

On the last planet in the Rigel system, the hypercharged ions of rain ease telepathic transmission, so that language is not needed for communication when it rains. Its color mirrors the mood of whoever it falls upon. When I was there on leave, feeling happy and relaxed, I ambled down the streets of its major city, glad to have a few days off and looking forward to seeing my family. I heard thunder; it started to shower, and I found myself awash in translucent skeins of green.

But suddenly someone bumped into me, and as he apologized his hand brushed my hip. I walked on, then decided to stop for lunch at a small cafe ahead, and checked my hippac to see if I had enough credits. It was gone! I searched everywhere, then realized I had been robbed.

The green-lit rain surrounding me changed into an opaque black shower that blocked the daylight, and I stumbled on for hours till I found my way home.

* * *

And there was my co-pilot, a woman who turned informer and was caught, turned into rain at the Penal Experimental Colony on the Venusian satellites. Her whole body was softened into a gel, then evanesced into water, until she could not move but only flow in one direction, wherever they chose to put her—to nourish whatever Earth-like planet's soil they decided to place her on.

And she cannot see or hear or smell, but only experience herself as torrents of surging water falling from an alien sky to serve the soil of some far-off world. She forgot her crimes, but forgot her delight in them also, to become a new memory in the mind of its people, the startlingly cool memory known as rain.

Speculative Poem

If we cut open the night,
reveal
the wounded darkness.
The stars
white gashes in the sky.
The opened sutures
where space was traumatized.
Silence is silver.
The women and the select
understand this equation.
Do not deny it.
Nor the green and red thunder.
Do not deny it. You know that
you see it too.
Take my pain for this laceration.
It is all I can offer you.

Remedios Varo

Remedios Varo, Remedios Varo, you were
Cloistered in your spiral city in Mexico,
Enspiralled into yourself, confined to vision,
Painting fantastic worlds beyond
The city you'd never leave.

You painted yourself free
Of the one place you couldn't flee—
Mexico City, "the Surrealist place,"
Haven for artistic refugees.
Your friends, Leonora and Max Ernst, lived there also,
And another Mexican woman artist, Frida Kahlo.

Bird-faced, bird-eyed
Owl-woman, you flew from Europe,
Another woman abandoning
Surrealism and its men—
Free to seek hierophany
In the sacred space of a new geography.

You painted impossibilities:
Machineries of magic
Fueled by heavenly ether, stardust and music;
And the science of the occult:
Alchemy and astronomy,
The physics of metaphysics,
Medieval mystics and psychoanalysis,
The artist as scientist.

Under a courtier's velvet cape,
The center of the universe whirls.
A city erupts from the sea: image of creation
Spiraling moonward, hermetic, its single street furls.

The fabric of space-time runs through our bodies—
This moment, its invisible axis,
A chance meeting's triviality.

Remedios Varo, Remedios Varo,
Your hair curling into delicate mathematical equations,
Insubmissive plant—
Where does the spirit go?
The terrestrial mantle you are embroidering
Is one you should be entering:

Weave your lover in; he is your escape
From the convent school,
From Europe,
And Surrealism's male dictates.

Your painting shows the young girls sewing,
Imprisoned in their guarded tower—
They are the enforced weavers
Of history's old patterns;
Till one's errant needle intrudes a sensed design,
A new paradigm,
Like love or scientific discovery,
Pure spirit, to help her flee
Into the freedom of destiny.

Her lover waits outside, as she weaves him within here.
But, once out, how to attain the higher sphere?
Stitch what cloth to leave Earth, shed this mortal mantle?
Find the lover beyond, the lover who is astral?

The Air

The air is a globe
made out of globes
that comes through the window
like a cat

Asking no more than to have
its presence acted upon

As the eye acts upon a face,
the heart to blood,
the blue flower of the brain
to light's angry scrawls.

Clear Thinking on Nebulous Issues

from an article in Discover *magazine*

This fast wind, with speeds up to 3,000 miles per second
Slams into the slow wind with the force
Of a trillion one megaton H-bombs—
Some red giants lose an entire sun's worth of matter this way.

It is a tale of galactic fireworks,
Rivaled only by the apocalypse of supernovas:
The real planetary nebula zoo.

Most stars will be blown away by the winds of change—
And their gravestones will be the planetary nebulas.

Astronomers have learned to read in these glowing fossils
The history of the winds,
The history of the stars from which they came.

Speculations

We are conspiracies of parallel universes;
Entangled, lovemaking proteins, filaments of blood-brocade;
Quantum instruments for star perception;
Tsunami time waves, future memories merging with predictions of the past;
Surging, fiery electrical impulses web-jumping our galaxy-festooned brains;
The collision of deviant, occult winds and strange crazewater.

Poem

A black hole's a fine and private place,
But none, I think, do there embrace.

Biographical Note

Lorraine Schein is a New York poet and writer whose work has appeared in *2001: A SF Poetry Anthology, Full Unit Hookup, The Beltane Papers, Strange Horizons , Gargoyle, Semiotexte SF, Terminal Velocities, StarLine,* and *Space and Time.* Her stories are included in the anthologies *Wild Women* and *Angel Body and Other Magic for the Soul* (Wordcraft of Oregon) and in *Alice Redux* (Paycock Press), a collection of stories about Alice in Wonderland. The *Raw Brunettes*, her novelette, was also published by Wordcraft.

Other books from Mayapple Press

Science fiction and fantasy poetry titles:

Judith Kerman and Don Riggs, eds.,
Uncommonplaces: Poems of the Fantastic, 2000
Paper, 148 pp, $15 plus s&h
ISBN 0-932412-17-3
David Lunde, *Blues for Port City,* 1995
Paper, 24 pp, $5 plus s&h
ISBN 0-932412-07-8

Other recent titles:

Rhoda Stamell, *Detroit Stories,* 2006 - our first fiction title!
Paper, 102 pp, $18.50 plus s&h
ISBN 0-932412-38-6
Douglas M. Smith, Melody Vassoff and Karen Woollams, eds.
In Drought Time: Scenes from Rural and Small Town Life, 2005
Paper, 110 pp, color illustrations, $24.95 plus s&h
ISBN 0-932412-37-8
Diane Shipley DeCillis & Mary Jo Firth Gillett, eds.
Mona Poetica: A Poetry Anthology, 2005
Paper, 114 pp, $16.50 plus s&h
ISBN 0-932412-36-X
Suzanne Keyworth, *Markers,* 2005
Paper, 72 pp, $14.95 plus s&h
ISBN 0-932412-35-1
Lidia Torres, *A Weakness for Boleros,* 2005
Paper, 48 pp, $12.50 plus s&h
ISBN 0-932412-34-3
Conrad Hilberry, *The Fingernail of Luck,* 2005
Paper, 32 pp, $10 plus s&h
ISBN 0-932412-33-5
Margo Solod, *Some Very Soft Days,* 2005
Paper, 84 pp, $15.50 plus s&h
ISBN 0-932412-32-7
John Palen, *Open Communion, 2005*
Paper, 98 pp, $16 plus s&h
ISBN 0-932412-31-9

For a complete catalog of Mayapple Press publications, please visit our website at *www.mayapplepress.com*

Books can be ordered direct from our website with secure online payment using PayPal, or by mail (check or money order).

Or order through your local bookseller.